W9-ASR-779

DATE DUE

BUILDING AMAZING STRUCTURES

Dams

NEW EDITION

Chris Oxlade

Heinemann Library
Chicago, Illinois

© 2006 Heinemann Library
a division of Reed Elsevier Inc
Chicago, Illinois

Customer Service 888-454-2279

Visit our website at www.heinemannraintree.com

Designed by Celia Floyd and Richard Parker (2nd edition)
Illustrations by Barry Atkinson
Originated by Modern Age
Printed and bound in China by WKT Company Ltd

10 09 08 07 06
10 9 8 7 6 5 4 3 2 1

Library of Congress Cataloging-in-Publication Data
Oxlade, Chris.
  Dams / Chris Oxlade.-- 2nd ed.
      p. cm. -- (Building amazing structures)
  Includes index.
  ISBN 1-4034-7903-8 (library binding-hardcover)
  1. Dams--Juvenile literature. 2. Dams--Design and construction--Juvenile literature. I. Title. II. Series.
  TC540.O95 2006
  627'.8--dc22

                        2005024037

Acknowledgments
The publishers would like to thank the following for permission to reproduce photographs: Ancient Art and
Architecture Collection p. **6**; Bill Hughes p. **20**; Corbis pp. **5**, **29**; Environmental Images pp. **22** (Omar
Sattaur), **26** (Alex Smailes), **27** (Toby Adamson); Hutchison Library pp. **12** (Robert Aberman), **16**, **18**,
19 (Robert Aberman), **23**; J. Allan Cash pp. **7**, **8**, **17**; James Davis Photography p. **11**; KATZ p. **15**;
Tony Stone pp. **4** (Peter/Steff Lamberti), **10** (Chris Swartz), **25** (Ary Diesendruck).

Cover photograph of the Hoover Dam in Nevada reproduced with permission of Lonely Planet.

Every effort has been made to contact copyright holders of any material reproduced in this book. Any
omissions will be rectified in subsequent printings if notice is given to the publishers.

The paper used to print this book comes from sustainable resources.

Contents

Some words are shown in bold. **like this**. You can find out what they mean by looking in the glossary.

About Dams

A dam is a huge barrier across a river that blocks the flow of river water. The water builds up behind the dam, making an artificial lake called a **reservoir**.

A dam is a type of structure. A structure is a thing that is built to resist a push or pull. A dam is a structure because it supports the immense wall of water in the reservoir behind it.

The biggest structures ever built are dams. Some are as high as a skyscraper or as heavy as a mountain, some make reservoirs as big as seas, and some make enough electricity for whole cities.

So why do we build dams? What different types of dams are there? How are they built? What special materials and machinery are needed?

Here we see the 725-foot (221-meter) high concrete **arch** of the Hoover Dam, and Lake Mead, the reservoir behind it. They are on the Colorado River, on the border between Arizona and Nevada.

The Grand Coulee Dam in Washington is a large concrete dam. Its hydroelectric power station is on the left.

Why do we build dams?

All dams do the same job, which is to hold back water. Sometimes the water is used for water supply and **irrigation**. Sometimes the water is used to produce electricity for homes, offices, and industry. The water flows down from the reservoir into a **hydroelectric power** station, where it turns **turbines** and **generators** that produce electricity.

Some dams are built to prevent flooding around a river **downstream** of the dam during heavy rains. The great rush of flood water collects behind the dam and is released gradually into the river below the dam. Some dams are designed to make a river deeper, so that ships can travel up and down the river.

FACTS ✤ It's a world record!

- Dam with the highest volume of material in its structure: Syncrude **Tailings,** Alberta, Canada. Completed: 1992. Volume: 706 million cubic yards (540 million cubic meters)—enough material to make a heap nearly 3 kilometers (2 miles) high!

- In 2003, water began to build up behind the Three Gorges Dam in China. When this dam is completed in 2009 it will be the world's largest. The reservoir will be 385 miles (620 kilometers) long.

Dams in the Past

People have been building dams for thousands of years. Early dams were built in countries with very dry **climates**. They supplied water to growing cities and **irrigated** land so that more food could be grown for increasing populations. Huge **hydroelectric power** dams have only been built in the last hundred years.

This is a water outlet gate on an 8th-century dam in the Yemen. The dam wall is built from stone blocks.

Ancient dam builders

The Ancient Egyptians probably built the first dams more than 5,000 years ago across the River Nile. Later civilizations, such as the Babylonians and Assyrians, who lived in the area we now call the Middle East, also built dams. So did the Romans. These dams were heavy banks up to 100 feet (30 meters) high. They were made of vast amounts of earth or rock and built without modern machinery. Some used simple concrete for strength and waterproofing. Dam building also started in China and other parts of Asia more than 2,000 years ago.

New dams for new industries

In Northern Europe a few dams were built after the **Middle Ages** to supply water to towns, to water-powered mills and to canals. When the **Industrial Revolution** began in the late 18th century, huge quantities of water were needed for rapidly growing cities and new industries.

In the 19th century, **engineers** began to study how structures stay up. New materials, such as stronger **cements** and **reinforced concrete**, were developed and powered tools were invented.

This allowed much larger dams to be constructed safely, which could hold back **reservoirs** big enough to supply all the water that was needed.

This dam in Wales is one of the several 19th-century dams that supply water to the cities of central Britain.

FACTS ✛ Old dam details

- The first dam we know of was built in about 2900 B.C. to divert water from the River Nile in Egypt, for irrigation.
- The oldest dam still in use is a dam built from rocks about 23 feet (7 meters) high in Syria. It was built in about 1300 B.C.—3,300 years ago.
- The first hydroelectric power station was built at Appleton, Wisconsin, in 1882. Its electricity lit two mills and a house.

Types of Dam

Modern dams come in dozens of different shapes and sizes, but there are really only four types. Each resists the push from the water on its **upstream** face in a different way. At the bottom of a **reservoir** 328 feet (100 meters) deep, the push on the dam wall is about the same as you would feel if a family car was resting on the palm of your hand!

Gravity dams

Put simply, a **gravity** dam is just an enormously heavy wall of concrete. The immense weight of the water cannot push the dam along or topple it over. The Grand Coulee Dam in Washington state contains a staggering 20 million tons of concrete.

Arch dams

An **arch** dam has a thin concrete wall which curves out into the reservoir. The push of the water goes around the dam to the sides and into the valley sides.

Many dams, such as this one in Nigeria, are made up of different types of dam joined end to end. This dam has an embankment dam at each end, and a gravity dam in the centre.

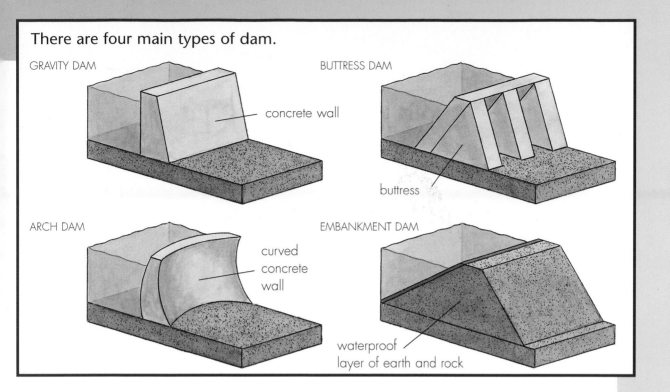

There are four main types of dam.

GRAVITY DAM

concrete wall

BUTTRESS DAM

buttress

ARCH DAM

curved concrete wall

EMBANKMENT DAM

waterproof layer of earth and rock

Buttress dams

A **buttress** dam has a sloping upstream face. The water pushes downwards and forwards on the face. The downwards push presses the dam into the ground, which helps it resist the forwards push. Heavy walls called buttresses support the **downstream** face to stop the dam toppling over.

Embankment dams

An **embankment** dam is a huge earth or rock bank, with gently sloping faces. It works like a combined gravity and buttress dam, but needs to be many times thicker than both. Earth and rock are not watertight like concrete, so an embankment dam needs a layer of waterproof material on the upstream face, or inside, to stop water seeping through.

TRY THIS
Feel the force
Stand two empty boxes on a flat surface about 4 inches (10 centimeters) apart. Put a plastic bag between the boxes. Slowly pour water into the bag. Eventually the boxes will move because of the push of the water. You can feel the push by trying to move the boxes together again. The deeper the water in the bag, the bigger the push will be.

Parts of a Dam

The main part of every dam is the dam wall itself, which holds back the water in the **reservoir**. The wall is usually a very simple structure, made from **reinforced concrete,** earth or rock. Other parts of a dam control the flow of water from the reservoir into the river **downstream** of the dam, into water supply pipes or into a **hydroelectric power** station. A power station is often part of the dam structure.

Monster water chutes

All dams have a **spillway** which works like a safety valve, letting water out of the reservoir when the water level rises too high. If there was no spillway, the water would eventually flow over the top of the dam and cascade down the downstream face. This would **erode** the base of the dam, perhaps causing it to collapse.

Some dams have a huge **turbine** hall in a cave blasted out of solid rock. Here turbines are being installed.

Spillways like these on the Itaipu Dam, on the Brazil-Paraguay border, handle the equivalent of several swimming pools of water every second, traveling at up to 62 miles (100 kilometers) per hour.

The spillway is either a channel in the downstream face of the dam, a channel at the side of the dam, called a chute, or tunnels blasted through the rock next to the dam.

Supplying water

Dams always have a system of pipes which allow water from the reservoir to flow straight into the river downstream, into the water supply system, **irrigation** channels or a hydroelectric power station. The inlets to this system are called intakes.

Bypassing the dam

A dam obviously blocks the river, stopping craft from moving along it. Where the river is an important waterway, canal **locks** are built to allow ships to move between the river below the dam and the new reservoir. Some dams also have a series of pools called a fish ladder, which allows fish to bypass the dam by leaping from pool to pool.

Holding up the dam

All dams must have solid foundations to support their massive weight. The foundations are normally made of **bedrock**. Although rocks are solid, most of them do let water seep through, sometimes through cracks and sometimes between the small particles which make up the rock. To stop water seeping through the rock foundations, a dam has a waterproof barrier underneath called a **cut-off**, often made with **grout**.

Dam-building Materials

The most important material for modern dam-building is concrete. The ingredients of concrete are **cement**, water, and aggregate, which is a mixture of sand and gravel. When the ingredients are first mixed, the concrete is liquid. The cement reacts with the water and then hardens into a solid which holds the aggregate together. Concrete is good for building because it is cheap and enormously strong. In fact, a piece of concrete about 4 inches (10 centimeters) square could support a 30-ton weight. Concrete can easily be shaped by pouring it into molds before it sets.

Reinforced concrete and steel are used to build a water intake on a dam in Turkey.

Adding super-strong steel

Concrete is extremely strong when it is squashed, or compressed. But when stretched, it cracks quite easily. Steel is immensely strong when it is stretched. For example, a steel cable only as thick as your finger could lift a 30-ton weight. Where part of a concrete structure will be stretched, steel bars are added to it. The new material is called **reinforced concrete**.

Watertight

Dam-builders often need to use special types of cement in their concrete to make it waterproof and stop **seepage**, or to make it resistant to attack by chemicals in the river water. Cement and water are also used to make a material called **grout**.

TRY THIS

Looking at seepage

Put a layer of sand 0.4 inch (1 centimeter) thick in the bottom of a tray. Use more sand to build up a model valley. Put a block of wood across the valley to act as a dam. Pour water onto the sand behind the dam to make a reservoir. Can you see how the water seeps through the sand under the wood? This is what would happen to a dam if the ground underneath was not grouted.

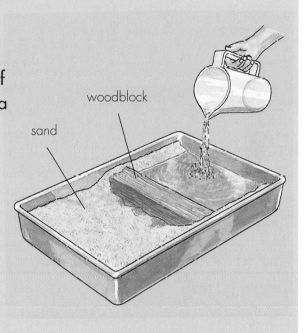

sand

woodblock

Natural materials

Embankment dams are built from materials such as chunks of solid rock, gravel, sand or clay. Materials with very small particles, such as clay, are used as a waterproofing layer.

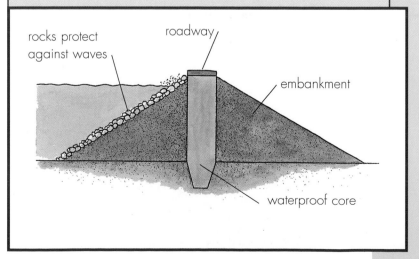

This is a cross-section of an embankment dam showing the waterproofing structure.

rocks protect against waves

roadway

embankment

waterproof core

Designing a Dam

Dams are built for large organizations. For example, an electricity supply company might want to build a dam to generate electricity, or a water supply company might want to build a dam to provide extra water. They hire a team of **engineers** to work on the design and construction of the dam. A **consulting engineer** oversees the project.

How big?

The engineers need to think about many different factors before deciding on the size of the dam. For example, if the dam is to produce electricity, it must be high so that the **reservoir** is deep and water rushes into the **turbines** with plenty of energy. These are called **hydroelectric** dams. If the dam is for water supply or flood control, the dam can be lower and longer so that it creates a large reservoir.

Where to build?

The site chosen will depend on its suitability for the construction of the dam itself and on the effects the reservoir will have when it is full of water. A **geological survey** of the ground around the site will tell the engineers whether the ground will support

What if an earthquake strikes?

Designers always investigate the **seismic** activity of a dam site. Earthquakes can crack a dam, making it leak or even collapse. This could cause catastrophic flooding. Tests and simulations on a computerized model of the dam help engineers tell what would happen if an earthquake struck a dam they are designing.

the weight of the dam and whether the rock is waterproof. The survey is done by digging **boreholes** to get samples of rock from deep underground.

What sort of dam?

The type of dam chosen depends on the width and depth of the valley and the **geology** of the site. **Embankment** dams are normally built in broad valleys where the **bedrock** is buried under layers of soft ground such as **silt** and clay, and where the cost of a concrete dam would be too high. Concrete dams are normally built in narrow valleys where the bedrock is near the surface.

This is a model of the design of the Three Gorges Dam in China. Models like this help engineers to explain the structure and workings of the proposed dam to non-engineers.

Preparing the Ground

Building a large dam is an enormous undertaking that can take thousands of workers more than ten years to complete. Usually one **engineering** company organizes the whole construction job. The dozens of special jobs, such as **grouting**, pipe work, or fixing steel reinforcements, are carried out by smaller companies.

Going underground

There is normally a lot of digging to do. Loose earth and rock must be removed to reveal the solid rocks that will form the foundations for the heavy dam. Trenches may need to be excavated to install waterproof **cut-offs** under the ground. If the rock allows water to seep through, holes are drilled and grout is pumped down them, from where it spreads into the ground and sets.

Before digging starts, a channel or tunnel is dug around the side of the site and the river is diverted to flow through it.

On the Itaipu Dam on the Brazil-Paraguay border, 50 million tons of rock had to be dug up just to create a diversion channel for the river.

Earth-moving monsters

Giant earth-moving machines do the digging work. Excavators dig down into the ground with a room-sized bucket, pulling up more earth in one go than a person could shovel in day. Bulldozers push loose earth and rock about, and loaders pick it up and drop it into dump trucks. These massive trucks can be as tall as a house. Where solid rock needs to be removed, it is broken up with explosives first.

These loaders and trucks are moving earth and rock at the site of the Gubi Dam in Nigeria.

TRY THIS

Firm foundations

Fill a container, such as a large margarine tub, with sand or earth and smooth the top over. Put the tub outdoors. Stand an empty plastic bottle on top of the sand. Gradually fill the bottle with water. As the bottle becomes heavier, the sand settles under it. This is what happens under a concrete dam as more and more concrete is added.

Building the Dam

Once the ground works are completed, work on the structure of the dam itself can begin. Large concrete dams contain a mind-boggling amount of concrete. Thirty million tons of it were used in the Itaipu Dam on the Brazil-Paraguay border. Delivering this much **ready-mixed concrete** would have taken two trucks a minute, 24 hours a day, for a whole year! So concrete-making plants are built at the site, and the concrete is carried into place in containers hanging from overhead cables. As the dam wall itself goes up, other parts of the dam, such as the **spillways** and **hydroelectric power** station, are constructed too.

Concrete and more concrete

Before any concrete is mixed, a mold must be made for it to be poured into. The mould is made with wooden sheets or steel plates, called **formwork**, supported by scaffolding. The reinforcing steel is put in place so that it will be encased when the concrete sets. The formwork stays in place until the concrete is set.

A concrete dam is built up in layers, and each layer is allowed to set before the next is added. The concrete is also covered with plastic sheeting to keep it from drying too quickly, which would make it crack.

Reinforcing steel and formwork can be seen at the top of this concrete dam wall.

Moving the earth

Millions of tons of earth and rock are needed to build an **embankment** dam, and dozens of massive earth-moving machines are needed. Earth and rock are quarried, transported to the site in monster trucks and tipped on the embankment. Each fresh layer is compacted (pressed down firmly) by heavy rolling machines to make it more waterproof and to stop it from being squashed by the weight of the layers above.

As the embankment rises, rocks or concrete blocks, often as big as cars, are added to the **upstream** face to protect it from the waves.

The gigantic earth embankment of the Ataturk Dam in Turkey is built up by earth-moving machines.

Dams in Use

With the dam complete, the **reservoir** begins to fill with river water. It may take months or even years to reach its full depth. Then the dam can begin supplying water and producing electricity. Some reservoirs are also used for leisure activities, such as fishing or sailing.

Controlling the flow

Hydrologists (experts on how water is collected and used) control how the water flows out of the reservoir. They operate sluice gates which allow water into water supply pipes, or the **hydroelectric power** station, or straight into the river below the dam.

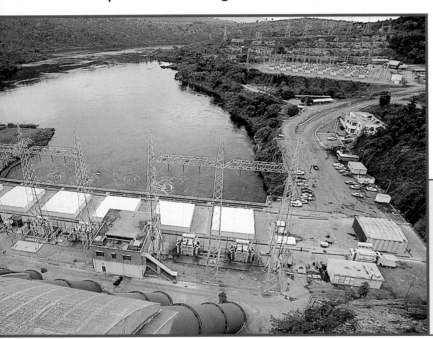

On the Akosomba Dam in Ghana, water flows downstream down huge pipes on the face, to the power station at the base of the dam.

Clearing the river

Allowing enough water into the river is important for the life in it and along its banks. It also stops the river from filling up with **silt.** Silt, or sediment, can build up because a dam reduces the natural flow of water. The slower the water flow, the more likely it is that silt will build up in the river channel. Occasionally a great rush of water is released to create a flood **downstream**. This helps to clear the river of silt.

Silt also settles at the bottom of the reservoir, leaving less room for the water. Most silt comes down the river during floods, so flood water is often allowed to flow out of the dam before the silt settles.

Spotting the cracks

A dam collapse can be a catastrophe because the whole reservoir full of water is released in one go. So the structure of a dam is constantly checked to make sure it is not moving or cracking. This is most important during the first few years after it has been completed. The ground under the dam and the reservoir can shift because of the added weight on top of it. Instruments inside the dam measure the forces on the dam and detect any tiny movements. The instruments can also tell designers if the structure is working as they thought it would.

TRY THIS

Taming a flood

This simple experiment shows how a finished dam helps with flood protection by storing a rush of flood water and releasing it gradually. Prop up one corner of a large, deep tray, such as a roasting pan, so that this corner is an inch or so (a few centimeters) higher than the opposite corner. Fill the tray with water until it overflows at the lowest corner. This represents a full reservoir. Now quickly pour a cup of "flood water" into the top corner. You should see that the water flows out of the bottom corner, but much more slowly.

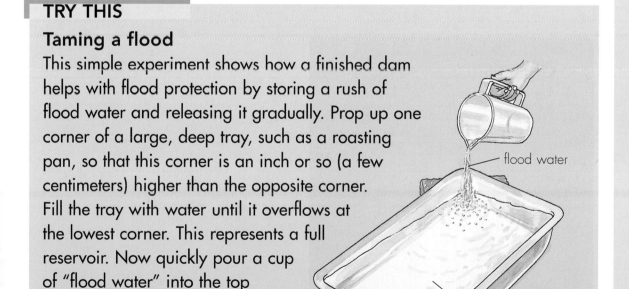

flood water

reservoir

water released slowly

Dam Programs

In the second half of the 20th century, hundreds of gigantic "superdams" were built on the major rivers of the world. These dams give huge benefits. They create reliable water supplies for cities and for farmers to grow their crops. They protect against floods and make the electricity needed for homes and industries. But these large dams may not be the best answer. **Environmentalists** argue that large dams do more harm than good because they destroy the natural flow of the river.

Anti-dam groups have tried to stop the construction of India's Sardar Sarovar Dam.

Problems at the Aswan Dam

The Aswan High Dam in Egypt was built during the 1960s to supply water for **irrigation** and to produce electricity. The dam cost about a billion dollars and took more than 10 years to build. It is an **embankment** dam 364 feet (111 meters) high, 2.4 miles (3.9 kilometers) long, and nearly 0.6 mile (1 kilometer) wide at its base. It contains enough rock to build 55 Great Pyramids. Lake Nasser, the dam's **reservoir,** is 14 miles (22 kilometers) across and almost 300 miles (500 kilometers) long.

By the 1980s, the farmers were using water from Lake Nasser to grow twice the amount of crops than before the dam was built, and the dam was creating a quarter of Egypt's electricity. A thriving fishing industry had grown up on Lake Nasser.

But the dam has had serious effects on the Nile **downstream**. **Nutritious silt** collects in Lake Nasser and no longer reaches the fields. Farmers have to use thousands of tons of artificial **fertilizers** instead, which have contaminated the river water, affecting fish and other life in the river. The Nile **Delta**, which was built up by silt from the river, is being flooded by the sea, and precious farmland is being lost.

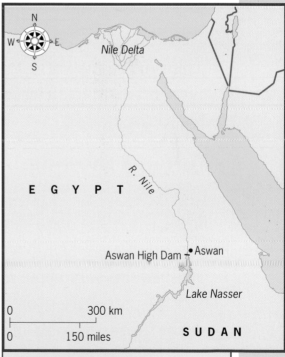

This is a map of the River Nile in Egypt, showing the Aswan Dam and Lake Nasser in the south, and the Nile Delta in the north.

23

Flood Defenses

Structures like dams help to prevent flooding of low-lying land next to rivers and along the coast. These flood-defense barriers are for keeping water out rather than for keeping it in.

Levees and dikes

Levees are **embankments** built alongside rivers keep water from spilling over the banks when flood water makes the water level rise. Dikes are similar, but protect low-lying coastal land from flooding by the sea. Levees and dikes are normally made of earth and are just several feet (a few meters) high. They must stand up to **erosion** from flowing water and waves.

Dikes are often used to reclaim land from the sea. A dike is built next to the coast to enclose an area of the sea. Then the sea water is pumped out, leaving a new area of land called a polder.

Turning the tide

Low-lying areas of land near coasts are threatened by storm tides, when the sea rises far above its normal level. A storm tide happens when there is a storm blowing towards the coast at the same time as there is a very high tide. Some coastal areas are protected by sea barriers, which stop storm surges flowing up **estuaries** and rivers.

A barrier has gates that are normally wide open, allowing river water to flow down to the sea, and sea water to flow in. This is what would happen naturally. But if a storm tide is forecast, the gates are closed against it, keeping the rising sea water out.

Power from the tide

A tidal barrage is like a two-way **hydroelectric power** dam across an estuary. As the tide rises, the water is deeper on the seaward side of the barrier. It flows through **turbines**, creating electricity. As the tide falls, the water flows back to the sea, creating electricity again

A tidal barrage creates power as sea water flows backwards and forwards through its turbines.

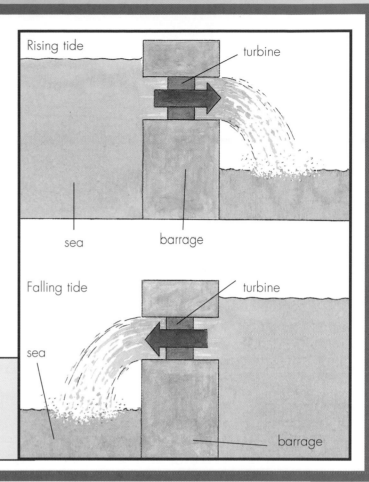

The Thames Barrier prevents flooding in low-lying areas of London. The underwater gates can be closed if there is a risk of flooding.

Dam Disasters

Ever since dams began to be built, some have collapsed, although this very rarely happens to large modern dams. When a dam collapses, the surge of water into the valley below is extremely destructive. Early dams, built mainly of earth, were often washed away as flood water flowed over the top. Others cracked during earthquakes. Modern dams are designed to withstand earthquakes and to let flood water through before it can flow over the top of the dam, but things can still go wrong.

The Guri Dam in Venezuela has not managed to prevent flooding of the surrounding countryside.

Calamitous collapses

The St. Francis Dam was a **gravity** dam north of Los Angeles. In 1928, it collapsed —as the **reservoir** filled, the pressure on the dam increased. Between 300 and 500 people were killed in the floods. The dam had been built on rock that moved because of the weight of the dam.

In 1975, the Banqiao Dam and Shimantam Dam, in Henan Province, China, collapsed. It is thought that 230,000 people died because of flooding, famine, and disease after the dams collapsed.

Killer wave

The 846-foot (258-meter) Vaiont Dam in the Italian Alps was completed in 1960. In 1963, flood water filled the reservoir to within 40 feet (12 meters) of the top of the dam. When a huge piece of the mountain above the reservoir slid into the water, it sent a wave as high as a 30-story building across the reservoir and over the dam. The water rushed down the valley below, flooding villages and drowning 2,500 people. Amazingly the **arch** dam survived intact.

Trouble ahead for the Three Gorges?

When it is completed in 2009, the enormous Three Gorges Dam on the Yangtze River in China will be the most powerful **hydroelectric** dam in the world. It will be 330 feet (100 meters) high and 1.2 miles (2 kilometers) long, and will create a reservoir 385 miles (620 kilometers) long. It will make 10 per cent of China's electricity and also protect the lower Yangtze from the floods that killed 300,000 people in the 20th century alone. Critics say that if the dam failed in an earthquake more than a million people would die—and earthquakes are common in the area. They believe that a series of small dams would be far safer.

Despite concerns, construction of the massive Three Gorges Dam in China continues.

Dam Facts

The world's tallest dams

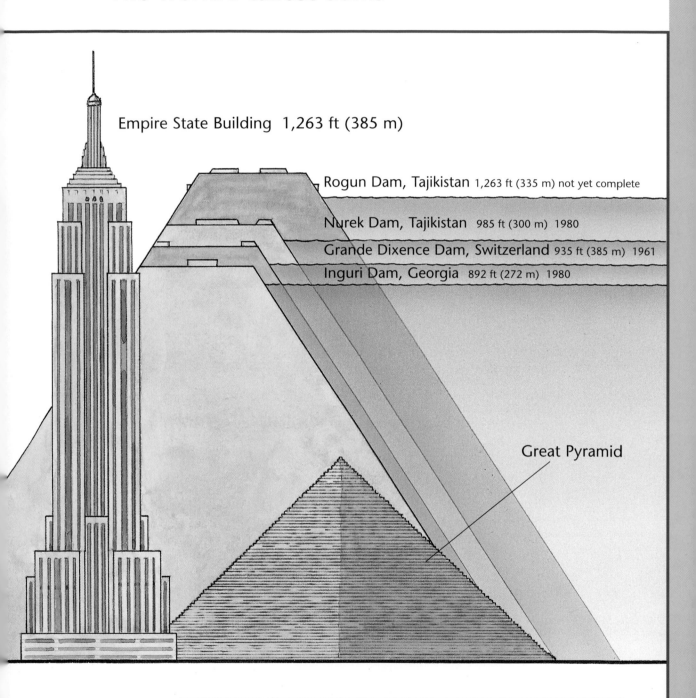

Empire State Building   1,263 ft (385 m)

Rogun Dam, Tajikistan 1,263 ft (335 m) not yet complete

Nurek Dam, Tajikistan 985 ft (300 m) 1980

Grande Dixence Dam, Switzerland 935 ft (385 m) 1961

Inguri Dam, Georgia 892 ft (272 m) 1980

Great Pyramid

The highest dams in the world would stand tall
against other incredible structures.

FACTS ✤ The world's biggest dams

(The dams which have used most materials to build them)

DAM	VOLUME		YEAR COMPLETED
	(MILLIONS OF CUBIC YARDS)	(MILLIONS OF CUBIC METERS)	
Syncrude **Tailings**, Alberta, Canada	706	540	1992
Chapeton, Argentina	387	296	under construction
Pati, Argentina	300	230	under construction
New Cornelia Tailings, Arizona	275	209	1973
Tarbela, Pakistan	165	126	1976

FACTS ✤ The world's most powerful hydroelectric dams

Power is measured in megawatts (MW). One MW lights about 20,000 light bulbs.

DAM	POWER (MW)	YEAR COMPLETED
Itaipu, Brazil/Paraguay	12,600	1983
Guri, Venezuela	10,300	1986
Tucurui, Brazil	7,690	1984
Grand Coulee, USA	6,495	1942
Savano-Shushenk, Russia	6,400	1983

The Guri Dam in Venezuela is the world's third most powerful dam.

Glossary

arch   type of structure that curves upwards or backwards over an opening

bedrock   layers of hard, solid rock that are found in the Earth's surface and continue deep into the Earth's crust

borehole   deep, narrow hole bored down into the ground to take samples of the earth and rocks below

buttress   supporting wall built at an angle to the wall it supports

cement   mixture of materials that hardens into a rock-like substance after it is mixed with water

climate   average pattern of weather for a large area

consulting engineer   engineer who decides how a structure should be built

cut-off   trench underneath a dam filled with waterproof material that keeps water seeping under the dam

delta   new land created by material deposited at the mouth of the river

downstream   further down a river, in the direction it is flowing

embankment   bank with a flat top and sloping sides built by piling up earth and rock

engineer   person who designs or builds a structure

environmentalist   person who works to protect the natural environment

erosion   process by which water and wind wear away artificial structures such as dams

estuary   area at the end of a river where it widens as it flows into the sea

fertilizer   material containing nutrients that is added to soil to help plants to grow

formwork   metal or wooden molds that concrete is poured into

generator   device similar to an electric motor – it creates electricity when its central core is spun round

geological survey   investigation to find out what layers of soil and rocks are under the ground

geology   study of rocks and how they are formed

gravity   the force that tries to pull every object towards every other object

grout   mixture of cement and water that is used to make earth or loose rock waterproof

hydroelectric power   power, normally in the form of electricity, made by letting water from a reservoir flow through a turbine

Industrial Revolution period in history from about 1750 to about 1850, when great advances in industry were made

irrigation collecting water and making it flow to where it is needed to water growing crops

lock step on a canal which allows ships to move uphill and downhill

Middle Ages time in European history between A.D. 500 and 1500

nutritious containing plenty of chemicals called nutrients, which are needed for plant or animal growth

ready-mixed concrete concrete that is mixed at a concrete mixing plant and transported to a construction site in a truck

reinforced concrete concrete that has steel reinforcing bars embedded in it

reservoir artificial lake which forms behind a dam

seepage water that trickles through the ground under or around a dam, or through an earth dam

seismic to do with earthquakes

silt very fine soil washed down a river and deposited at its mouth

spillway chute that allows excess reservoir water to flow safely over or around a dam

tailings dam containing a reservoir of water and sludge pumped from mine workings. It is built from the waste material dug from the mine.

turbine wheel that is turned by flowing water. In a hydroelectric power station, water flowing down from the reservoir turns turbines which turn generators.

upstream further up a river, in the opposite direction to the way a river is flowing

More Books to Read

Doherty, Craig A., Katherine M. Doherty, and Bruce Glassman (Editor). *Hoover Dam*. Woodbridge, Conn.: Blackbirch Press, Incorporated, 1995. An older reader can help you with this book.

Gresko, Marcia S. *Grand Coulee Dam*. Woodbridge, Conn.: Blackbirch Press, 1999.

Index